GREEK BY HERITAGE
ITALIAN BY HEART

Marcia Georges

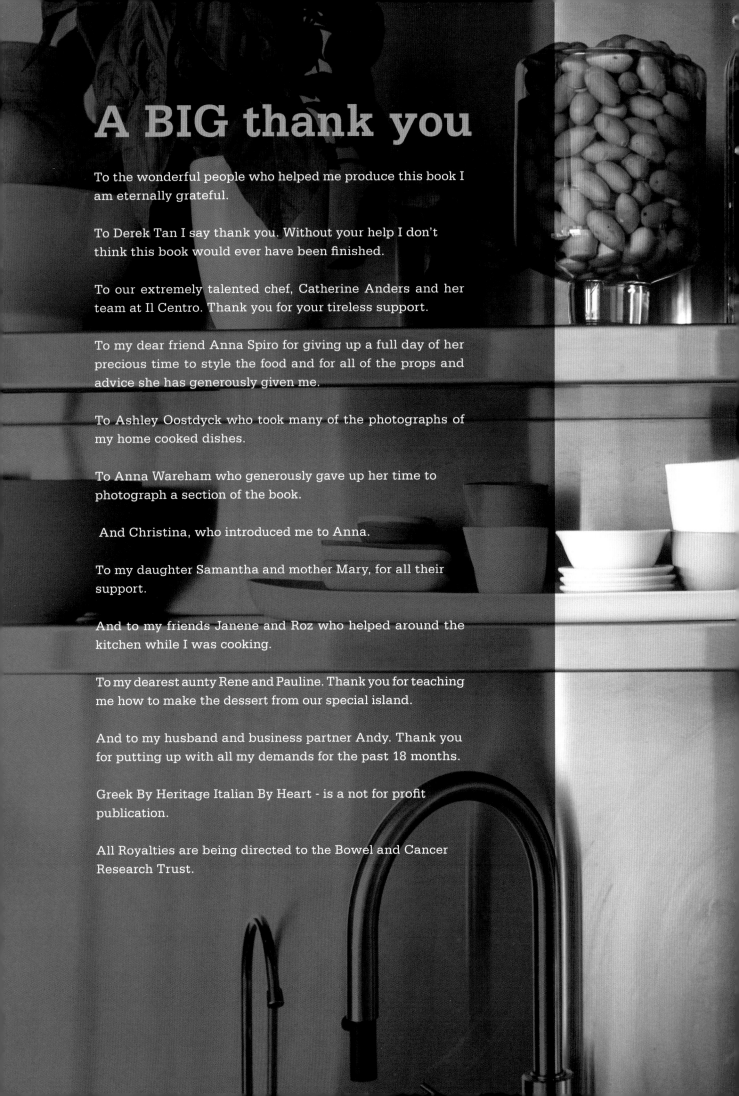

A BIG thank you

To the wonderful people who helped me produce this book I am eternally grateful.

To Derek Tan I say thank you. Without your help I don't think this book would ever have been finished.

To our extremely talented chef, Catherine Anders and her team at Il Centro. Thank you for your tireless support.

To my dear friend Anna Spiro for giving up a full day of her precious time to style the food and for all of the props and advice she has generously given me.

To Ashley Oostdyck who took many of the photographs of my home cooked dishes.

To Anna Wareham who generously gave up her time to photograph a section of the book.

And Christina, who introduced me to Anna.

To my daughter Samantha and mother Mary, for all their support.

And to my friends Janene and Roz who helped around the kitchen while I was cooking.

To my dearest aunty Rene and Pauline. Thank you for teaching me how to make the dessert from our special island.

And to my husband and business partner Andy. Thank you for putting up with all my demands for the past 18 months.

Greek By Heritage Italian By Heart - is a not for profit publication.

All Royalties are being directed to the Bowel and Cancer Research Trust.

A labour of love

I've always had a passion for good food. I guess growing up in Brisbane as the daughter of a Greek restaurateur, you could say cooking good food is in my blood.

One thing that I have learned over my fortunate life is that good food and good times go hand in hand. So I've always wanted to create a cookbook made up of the dishes that are close to my heart.

This cookbook has been a lifetime in the making. It shares dishes I remember fondly from my childhood; recipes I've enjoyed through my family holidays in Greece; and of course, some of my favourite recipes developed with my husband as the owners of our own establishment, Il Centro Restaurant.

In the 21 years we have been operating Il Centro, we have remained loyal to many of our suppliers. These wonderful people listed below have supported me to raise money for my charity Cancer and Bowel Research Trust via this publication.

VISCO SELECTED FINE FOODS

SAMUEL SMITH & SONS, NEGOTIANTS WINES

MOET HENNESSY AUSTRALIA

GRINDERS COFFEE PTY LTD

SIMON GEORGE AND SONS PTY LTD

DEEP BLUE FISHERIES

ROCCO SEAFOODS

DELTA HOSPITALITY PTY LTD

PALATABLE PARTNERS

I am delighted to share my recipes with you. While my family has shared many great times, we have also known our share of grief due to cancer. So by purchasing my book you are helping this wonderful charity and maybe we can help find a cure for this terrible disease.

Please enjoy my recipes

Marcia Georges

cancer & bowel research trust

CONTENTS

THE EARLY YEARS

I grew up in Brisbane in the late 1950s the youngest daughter of a first generation Australian-born mother and a Greek father.

My dad, Michael Karlos, was a cook/cafe owner and somewhat of a pioneer in the restaurant industry. I remember whenever we sat down to a family meal, the conversation at the dinner table would always work its way around to how the meal was prepared and how it could be improved. Dad would always comment on the quality of the produce, especially how fresh it was.

Food was a very serious topic of conversation in our house.

I have fond memories of playing pretend games with my older sisters, Pauline and Diane. One of our favourite games was "cafes". One of us would be the cook, another a waitress, while the other would sit with our collection of dolls (and often our dog Sally), and pretend to be customers. We were never satisfied with only one customer, the cafe had to be busy, just like our father's.

We played this game a lot, but never when friends came over. Having a Greek cafe owner father was a bit embarrassing back then.

The 50s and 60s were busy times for my father. Over this time he grew from small cafe proprietor to large cafe proprietor, to award winning a-la-carte restaurant owner - one of only a few in Brisbane! He really was an enterprising man; a visionary well ahead of his time.

Michael owned and operated the Liberty Cafe in Stanley Street, Woollongabba. Soon after, he opened the Astoria Cafe in the city - with entrances in Adelaide & Edward Streets. But Michael's career began to take off in 1954 when he opened the Carolena Coffee Lounge in Queen Street, opposite the GPO. Three years later he opened a second coffee lounge, the Cubana, a block away in Albert Street.

Having introduced the first espresso coffee machines to Brisbane, my father's coffee lounges proved very popular.

Camelia · a family affair

George Tambarkis married the boss's daughter, followed this up by buying the boss' restaurant, and you'll find him in the spotlight flaming garlic prawns at the Camelia.

The Camelia is one of the longest-living restaurants in town, and is downstairs at the top end of Queen Street.

It was opened by Michael Karlos, who runs the Top of the State in 1956, and was the fifth restaurant in Queensland to get a licence.

George at this time was busy completing a six year apprenticeship as an electrician. His father, who came to Australia from Greece in 1924, was in the cafe business and had the Prince Consort in the Valley.

George then met Pauline, Michael Karlos' daughter, decided to leave the world of electricity to "spark up things in the restaurant business."

He started as a waiter, then graduated to head waiter, assistant manager and then general manager of his father-in-law's business.

Two years ago in partnership with Andy Georges, a former accountant, and another of Mr. Karlos's sons-in-law, he bought the Cubana Coffee lounge in Albert Street, and the Camelia.

Now the restaurants take up their lives, "and our wives and families complain they don't see enough of us."

The Camelia is open every day except Sunday, and on Friday and Saturday nights until 11 p.m.

There are three cooks under a Greek chef, and the international flavour is quite something with a head waiter, Walter

Rusich, an Italian from Trieste "so almost a Yugoslav," a Danish barman and a Dutch waiter.

The Camelia has just been equipped with a smart black and white bar which cuts their dining area down, but pleases the clients.

The room itself is slightly Japanese, with black saucer lights set into a white ceiling and Japanese screens, that are lit from the back illuminating pressed butterflies and flowers.

❖❖❖

There's a big, new menu, with separate and special ones for lunch and dinner. There's another for the sweets.

George who is dapper in beautifully cut suits, is aiming for the business man trade at lunchtime, and "the young people at night." Portuguese pianist Dick de Rozario is there to do the serenading.

Those garlic prawns that George prepares with such aplomb are surely the most garlicky, alcoholic prawns in town. Served as an entree they're $1.95 As main meal, $3.25.

GEORGE TAMBARKIS

The menu offers cold meats, all sorts of fish and shell fish in season, every type of steak that can be cooked at the table, at $4 a piece, spaghetti carbonara, at $2.50 a large serving, and al...

Tribute to great Greeks

OUR State had a sad start to 1987 with the death of two great Queenslanders — Chris Sourris and Michael Karlos.

Honorary Consul-General for Greece Alex Freeleagus told me last week both men, who spent almost their whole lives in their adopted Australia — had blazed the way for the multicultural society.

Chris Sourris came from the island of Kythera in Greece to Goondiwindi in southwest Queensland in the 1920s.

He became a successful movie theatre operator, particularly in Tenterfield and Stanthorpe, and later with the Aspley and Capalaba Drive-Ins.

Immediately after World War II he started up Stanthorpe Turf Club, of which he was president.

He became a leader of Queensland's Greek community.

Over 40 years he raced any number of good horses including the 1960 Sydney Cup winner, Grand Garry.

At his death, he was still as vital as ever as he had purchased a yearling at the January 1987 New Zealand sales.

Michael Karlos was a dynamic restaurateur.

He obtained the first liquor licence for a restaurant in Queensland, at his Camelia in Queen St.

He also was the first owner of the Top of the State restaurant until he retired a few years ago.

He came from Castellorizo in Greece in the 1930s as did that other concerned Queenslander, Senator George Georges.

● **Kevin Driscoll OBE** is about to organise a Light Horse event to correspond with Australia's 1988 Bicentenary celebrations.

● He was surprised when I told him both **Len Hughes MBE**, former secretary of the Queensland Turf Club, and Sir Edward Williams of Elders Ltd., Expo, Commonwealth Games, Queensland Turf Club etc were members of the Light Horse before the Six Years War.

Camelia

introduces a new name in Brisbane's Restaurant luxurious surroundings; a new standard in satisfy the most fastidious Gourmet. Camelia also offers Espresso Coffee, Light Snacks. Reservations are available for special functions.

Camelia Restaurant, downstairs in the new Roubin Arcade, 117 Queen Street, is open Monday till Saturday from 9.30 a.m. to midnight. Fully Air-Conditioned.

CUBANA

● Lunching at the Camelia Room were Mrs. Michael Pherous of New Farm and Mrs. George Tambakis of Rainworth who have just returned from the Sydney wedding of their sister Marcia and Sydney boy Andy Georges. The girls are the daughters of

---

WATSON PLUMBING P...
508 Boundary St. Spring Hill...

THE **Carol...**

is
to welcome as o...
an exc...
air-conditioned resta...

the

We extend our Congratulation...
to the Management of

Camelia
RESTAURANT

Inspired by the popularity of his coffee lounges, Michael Karlos embarked on a more ambitious venture in 1959, opening his first restaurant. But not just any restaurant, The Camelia was to become one of only 10 restaurants in Queensland issued with a liquor licence.

The menu was labelled 'Continental cuisine' but featured quite a few Australian dishes - particularly for people resisting change. Remember, this was the late fifties, and the dining public's palette was very different to what it is today.

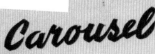

Opened in 1959, the Camelia was one of only two popular restaurants in Brisbane (well, not attached to a hotel). It attracted quite a reputation. Dignitaries, overseas travellers, local and interstate diners... not to mention visiting celebrities. It seemed anyone who was anyone would dine at the Camelia.

My father was very proud of his restaurant and had he been alive in 1992 when my husband Andy and I opened our restaurant, Il Centro, he would have been proud of that too.

I have lots of fond memories of my father's first restaurant. The recipes in the following section were always popular with diners at the Camelia. I know I always enjoyed eating them.

Calamari was quite an exotic dish in the early 60s. Michael often recommended calamari to his customers saying, "Baby squid is not bait!" I remember him repeating this time and time again to diners - even if they didn't ask.

I grew up eating octopus. So to me, the thought of someone being afraid to eat squid was ludicrous.

FRIED CALAMARI

with garlic sauce

INGREDIENTS

1kg squid

oil for frying

flour

GARLIC SAUCE

500g day old white bread

4 cloves of garlic

200ml extra virgin olive oil

juice of 1 lemon

salt and white pepper

METHOD

Clean squid or ask your fishmonger to clean for you and cut into 2cm rings. Tentacles can also be used but these will splash when cooking - beware!

Toss squid lightly in seasoned flour shaking to remove excess. In a shallow pan heat oil until very hot. Drop squid a few at a time in hot oil and cook until lightly coloured. Drain on kitchen paper and serve with a lemon cheek and garlic sauce on the side.

GARLIC SAUCE

Soak the white bread in a little water then squeeze out well. Blend the bread and garlic cloves in a blender, gradually adding the olive oil and lemon juice. Season with salt and pepper.

NOTE: Garlic sauce is thick and is best made the day before eating. Cooked potatoes can be used in place of white bread.

Serves 6.

LOBSTER MORNAY

INGREDIENTS

1 green lobster

SAUCE

½ cup fish stock

½ cup lite milk

1 bay leaf

5 peppercorns

½ onion

1 tbsp butter

1 tbsp plain four

1 tbsp dijon mustard

60g grated cheese

extra butter for lobster

METHOD

In a pan heat fish stock and lite milk with bay leaf and half an onion. Bring to the boil and then turn off heat, cover and allow liquid to infuse.

In another pan melt butter, add flour and stir carefully to make a roux. Add mustard and stir to combine. Remove from heat and slowly add warm liquid. Return to heat and stir carefully until combined and starting to thicken. Add grated cheese and set aside.

Cut lobster in half lengthways. Brush with a little butter and place under a hot grill. Grill for about 8 minutes until almost cooked. Spread mornay thickly on the lobster, sprinkle with remaining cheese and return to the grill. Cook until top is golden brown.

Serves 2.

Camelia's Steak Dianne was always prepared at the table with a lot of fanfare by the Maitre d' or head waiter.

STEAK DIANNE

INGREDIENTS

STEAK DIANNE

1kg beef eye fillet

1 tbsp black peppercorns, crushed

salt

50g butter

3 cloves garlic

¼ cup cream

4 tbsp Worcestershire sauce

½ cup Madeira (or other sherry)

finely chopped parsley

CREAMY MASHED POTATOES

6 medium sized potatoes

salt

25g butter

¾ cup of hot milk

white pepper

METHOD

STEAK DIANNE

Cut fillets into 1cm slices and pound until thin. Sprinkle each steak with salt and crushed pepper. Melt 1/2 butter in a large pan and gently fry steaks on both sides. Remove from pan and keep warm.

Add remaining butter to pan with crushed garlic and cook for a few seconds. Add Worcestershire sauce and Madeira and cook for 1 minute. Pour in cream and heat through without boiling. Return steaks to pan and cover with the sauce. Season to taste and sprinkle parsley on top.

CREAMY MASHED POTATOES

Peel potatoes and put into a saucepan with enough lightly salted cold water to cover. Cook with a lid on pan for 20–30 minutes. Drain thoroughly then shake the pan over heat making sure all the water has evaporated. Mash with a potato masher or put through a ricer.

Add butter to potatoes and beat with a wooden spoon until very smooth gradually adding the hot milk until potatoes are light and fluffy. Season with salt and pepper.

Serves 6.

CARPET BAG STEAK

INGREDIENTS

6 x 300g sirloin steaks

18 oysters

grated zest of ½ lemon

flat leaf parsley

salt and white pepper

METHOD

Trim steaks and cut a small pocket on one side of each steak. Season with salt. Toss oysters in lemon zest and a few roughly torn parsley leaves. Season with salt and white pepper. Stuff 3 oysters in each steak and secure with cooking twine. Pan fry or char-grill steaks.

Best when cooked rare or medium rare.
Remove cooking twine before serving.

Serves 6.

Although most think Eye Fillet should be used for Carpet Bag Steak, this is how I remember my dad's recipe.

The Camelia was very popular for its grilled Jewfish. Jewfish is not as readily available these days, so I like to use Snapper in this recipe.

28

GRILLED FISH

with lemon butter sauce

INGREDIENTS

FISH

4 x 200g servings
of snapper fillets
(skin removed)

oil to brush fish

salt

LEMON BUTTER SAUCE

200g butter

3 egg yolks

3 tbsp lemon juice

salt and white pepper

METHOD

FISH: Salt fish on both sides and brush with a little oil. Cook skinned side up for 2 minutes or until starting to colour. Turn over and cook for 3 minutes more. Place pan in a moderate oven while you make the sauce. Check often making sure not to overcook the fish.

LEMON BUTTER SAUCE: Melt butter over low heat. Do not brown. Remove from heat. Place egg yolks, lemon juice, sea salt and pepper in a food processor and process until pale and smooth. With processor running, pour in the melted butter in a slow, steady stream.

TO SERVE: Remove fish from oven and spoon over the sauce.

Serves 4.

LOBSTER THERMIDOR

INGREDIENTS

1 medium sized cooked
lobster

25g butter

1 small onion,
finely chopped

25g mushrooms
finely sliced

1 tbsp plain flour

100ml milk

1/8 teaspoon dry mustard

½ tsp salt

pinch of cayenne pepper

50ml cream

1 egg yolk

1 tbsp dry sherry

1 tsp lemon juice

50g grated cheese

METHOD

Cut lobster in half lengthways. Remove lobster meat and cut into neat slices following the marks of the joints. Wash, dry and reserve shell. Melt butter in a saucepan and gently fry onion and mushrooms for 2-3 minutes. Stir in flour and cook over a low heat for 1 minute

Add milk and bring to the boil over a medium heat stirring continuously. Add mustard, salt and cayenne pepper. Stir in cream, egg yolks, sherry, lemon juice and lobster meat.

Heat through and place mixture in lobster shells and sprinkle with grated cheese. Place under a heated grill and cook until golden brown.

Serves 2.

BOMBE ALASKA

BOMBE ALASKA

INGREDIENTS

1 35cm x 25cm sponge

½ cup brandy

500g fruit salad

6 scoops vanilla ice cream

MERINGUE

4 egg whites

75g caster sugar

1 vanilla bean, split

METHOD

MERINGUE: Whisk the egg whites slowly adding the sugar until firm peaks form. Scrape the vanilla pod and add to the mixture. Beat until mixture is thick and glossy.

FRUIT SALAD: Chop a variety of fruits of your choice into medium dice. Strain diced fruit to remove most of the juice and reserve juice. Flavour the fruit with a small amount of the brandy.

TO ASSEMBLE: Cut sponge to fit the base of a shallow dish. Sprinkle with 1/2 the remaining brandy. Pile on the fruit salad and ice cream creating a high mold. Moisten the remaining sponge cake with the reserved juice and brandy. Press around the mold to form a round "bombe". Using a large spatula cover it with a thin layer of meringue. Brown with a blowtorch. Heat extra brandy in a small saucepan. Ignite the brandy, pour over the bombe alaska and take to the table while in flame.

Serves 6–8

sponge

INGREDIENTS

1 35cm x 25cm baking dish

75g plain flour

150g self raising flour

6 eggs

220g caster sugar

2tbsp boiling water

METHOD

Preheat oven to 180C. Grease and line baking dish.

Sift flours together. Beat the eggs until thick and pale. Add sugar slowly, beating well. Fold the flour into the mixture using a metal spoon and add 2 tablespoons of boiling water.

Spread the mixture into the baking dish. Bake for 20 minutes.

Allow to cool for 5 minutes before turning out onto cooling rack.

vanilla ice cream

INGREDIENTS

300ml cream

900ml milk

330g castor sugar

10 egg yolks (reserve whites
to make meringue for bombe alaska)

1 vanilla bean

METHOD

Heat cream, milk, half the sugar and the vanilla bean – cut in half lengthways and scraped into liquid. Bring to the boil.

Whisk the yolks and remaining sugar until white and fluffy. Add hot liquid. Cool over iced water bath then churn in an ice cream churner for about 15 minutes.

Makes 2 litres.

CRÊPES SUZETTE

The Camelia was famous for Crêpes Suzette. I would often hear dad relaying to mum how many they had sold that day. Everyone enjoyed the experience of having the dish prepared and flamed at the table.

CRÊPES SUZETTE

INGREDIENTS

12 crêpes
(recipe follows)

SAUCE

4 sugar cubes

1 orange

75g unsalted butter

squeeze of lemon juice

½ cup grand marnier

½ cup brandy warmed

METHOD

Rub the sugar cubes on the rind of the orange until well flavoured. Crush the sugar with a fork and cream with 45g of butter.

In a frying pan, place the remaining 30g of butter. Add the orange and lemon juice along with the grand marnier and bring to the boil. Add the creamed orange butter and stir until dissolved.

Place the warm crêpes a couple at a time in the pan and spoon over sauce. Fold each crêpe over into a triangle and leave to one side of pan until all crêpes are done. Spoon the sauce over all the crêpes and sprinkle with warmed brandy.

Set alight and wait for flames to die before serving.

Allow 2 crêpes per person.

Serves 6.

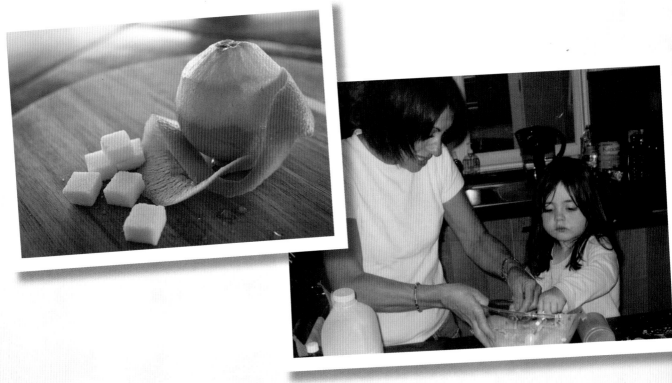

crêpes

INGREDIENTS

1¼ cups flour

pinch of salt

3 eggs beaten

1½ cups milk

1 tbsp brandy

1 tbsp melted butter

METHOD

Sift the flour and salt in a large mixing bowl. Make a well in the centre and stir in the eggs and milk. Mix well and add in the melted butter and brandy.

Cover and allow to stand for about 1 hr. If batter is too thick add more milk (batter should be thin like cream).

Heat an 18cm crêpe pan and pour in a little oil then wipe with a paper towel. Pour in about 2 tablespoons of batter and rotate pan to make a very thin crêpe. Place cooked crêpe over an inverted soup bowl. Continue making them until all batter is used placing each crêpe on top of the other.

Cover with a tea towel until ready to use.

Crêpes may be made ahead of time and stored in the refrigerator.

Makes about 20.

MEMORIES OF GREECE

While Dad was busy entertaining Brisbane with his 'Continental' cuisine, my mother, Mary was at home cooking delicious Greek food. Although Mum is born in Australia, she enjoyed cooking the Greek dishes of her heritage for the family.

Dad was born on the Greek island of Kastellorizo, the eastern most island of the Dodecanese in the Aegean Sea.

I love visiting Greece, but I especially love visiting Kastellorizo. 'Our Island' is closer to Turkey than it is to Greece and at night the colourful lights of the Turkish town of Kas can be clearly seen sparkling on the horizon. It's only a short boat ride to Kas. Many island visitors and residents from Cassie (the pet name for Kastellorizo) take the half day trip to Kas on Fridays to shop at the markets.

Turkey is very different to Greece and while I enjoy visiting Kas, I am always pleased to be on the boat in the afternoon returning to Kastellorizo.

I have so many wonderful memories of my time in Greece. The recipes in this section are reminders of the many Greek people and special occasions that have influenced my life.

My father would cook some of these on Saturday evening after a day at the races. We'd eat them at cocktail hour with a glass of champagne or gin martini.

Mum and I were never quite sure which drink was for celebrating a win and which was for commiserating a loss.

ALMOST GREEK
PAN-FRIED OYSTERS

INGREDIENTS

1 dozen oysters
(Dad used bottled oysters–
shucked oysters are
good here)

finely grated fresh white
breadcrumbs

butter

METHOD

Take oysters from their shells.

Coat them individually in the breadcrumbs.

In a small frying pan large enough to fit all the oysters snugly, melt the butter. Put all the oysters in the pan and cook gently on one side until lightly brown.

Invert a plate over the pan and turn out oysters then slide them back into the pan to cook the other side. Do not overcook. Slide them onto a serving plate and squeeze lemon over. Season with pepper

Delicious with chilled champagne.

FASOLADA

bean soup

INGREDIENTS

2½ cups dried lima beans
soaked overnight

1 large onion halved
and sliced

3 carrots, thinly sliced

2 stalks of blanched celery
including leaves, thinly
sliced

5 large tomatoes, skinned,
seeds removed and
chopped

1 generous cup Greek extra
virgin olive oil

¼ cup chopped parsley

salt

freshly ground black pepper

(as this a simple dish
it is necessary that the
vegetables are fresh and
of top quality)

METHOD

Drain the beans well and put them in fresh water and bring to the
boil then drain. Repeat this process twice. Place beans in 2 litres
of fresh water.

Add the remaining ingredients and cook over moderate heat for
about 1 hour. Season with salt and pepper, stir in chopped parsley.

Serve hot with crusty bread.

Serves entree 6 / main 4.

Easter is a very important festival in the Greek community. The first full moon of spring heralds the high point of the church year in the Greek Orthodox calendar. At this time, devout Christians fast for 40 days, forgoing meat, cheese and eggs. The less devout (I fall into this category) respect the fasting rules during "Holy Week", the week before Easter Sunday.

Although my family didn't follow the demanding traditions of the faithful, we did enjoy the food and celebrations, such as the traditional dyeing of red eggs on Maundy Thursday (the Thursday before Easter Sunday) and the Saturday midnight feast of fresh Easter soup, "Mayiritsa", to celebrate the resurrection of Christ.

Easter Sunday was always a family celebration with roast lamb - sometimes a whole lamb on the spit. And no Easter would be complete without my grandchildren's favourite, Koulourakia.

FAVA

split pea puree

INGREDIENTS

2 cups yellow split peas

8 cups vegetable stock
or water

1 onion chopped

1½ tsp salt

extra virgin olive oil

½ onion finely diced
and squeeze of lemon

METHOD

Wash split peas well discarding any that are discoloured. Place in
a large saucepan and cover with the cold stock or water. Bring to
the boil. Skim and add the chopped onion. Cover and simmer gently
without stirring until peas are very soft, approx 2 hours. Add more
water during cooking if necessary. Stir in salt.

TO SERVE: Ladle into serving bowls, top with diced onion,
a generous tablespoon of oil and wedge of lemon.

Serves 4.

I love Fava. Although it is traditionally eaten during the 40 days of fasting before Easter, I cook it all year round.

Revithopites are time consuming and messy to make so I can understand why the old Greek grandmothers loved to cook them. Unlike the modern day grandmother, they had nothing better to do with their time. I suggest you don't make these if you're running late for golf!

CHICK. PEAS

1 bowl of check Peas soaked in water O'Xernyt-
cruished Peas xd. 1 grated onion 4 Eshellets-
choped fine ½ bowl of Grated cheese ½ Cup-
Plain flauer. 1 egg. ¼ bowl of cream.
¼ cup of milk. 1 Table Spoon of chopped Parsley
1 Tab of chopped Mint Pepper & Salt. Blend
alltogether & fried in Hot oil.
Spoonful at a time until Golden.
Brown.

(ROTHO Peters)

REVITHOPITES

INGREDIENTS

1 cup chickpeas soaked
in water overnight

1 onion grated

4 shallots finely chopped

½ cup grated kefalograviera
cheese

½ cup plain flour

½ cup cream

¼ cup milk

¼ cup chopped parsley

½ cup chopped mint

salt and white pepper

oil for frying

METHOD

Drain chickpeas, put in a pan and cover with cold water. Bring to the boil. Cook until just tender. Mash slightly in a food processor but do not blend. Mix together with onion, shallots, cheese, parsley and mint. Stir in flour, milk and cream and mix well.

Using a nonstick frying pan heat the oil until very hot. Take a dessert spoon of mixture and drop into the hot oil. Flatten a little with the back of spoon.

Fry for 4 minutes each side don't allow to burn. If they break up don't worry as you can fix it when you flip it over.

Great served as a light lunch with a salad.

Make smaller revithopites (if you dare) to serve as cocktail food topped with a dollop of parsley pesto.

Makes about 30.

PARSLEY & ALMOND PESTO

INGREDIENTS

½ bunch curly leaf parsley

½ bunch continental parsley

1 garlic clove

pinch salt

100ml extra virgin olive oil

1/3 cup blanched almonds

25ml water

METHOD

Trim stalks off parsley and discard. Put parsley, chopped garlic and roughly chopped almonds into blender. Pulse for a few seconds then add salt. With motor running pour in oil in a steady stream until all combined.

Serve with revithopites or delicious tossed through hot pasta.

CHICKEN & SPAGHETTI

INGREDIENTS

1 whole chicken cut
into portions

1 onion diced

2 x 400g tinned
tomatoes chopped

2 cloves sliced garlic

2 tbsp tomato paste

1 cup red wine

½ cup water

½ cup chopped parsley

1 fresh bay leaf

salt & pepper

500g spaghetti

grated parmesan and
extra chopped parsley
to serve

METHOD

Heat some olive oil in a large pan. Toss chicken lightly in plain flour. Fry garlic and remove from pan when brown. Add onion and cook till transparent remove from pan and add chicken and brown on all sides cooking a few pieces at a time until all done. Deglaze pan with red wine. Return chicken with onion to pan, add tomatoes, tomato paste, bay leaf, parsley and water. Cook for ½ hour. Season with salt and pepper. In the meantime place a large saucepan of water on the stove to boil. When water is boiling rapidly, add spaghetti and cook until al dente.

TO SERVE: Divide spaghetti between 4 pasta bowls and sprinkle with the grated cheese. Add a portion of chicken and pour over some sauce. Top with chopped parsley.

All you need with this dish is a crisp lettuce salad, dressed with olive oil and lemon juice.

Serves 4.

Although Chicken & Spaghetti is a simple dish by today's standards, my dad's Chicken & Spaghetti was really special and became a family favourite. We always included this at special family celebrations.

Mum and Dad would visit their poultry supplier to make sure the chickens were very fresh, plump and always free range. Dad taught me very early on that "good quality produce always produces a good result!"

MY SIMPLE CHOPPED MIXED SALAD

INGREDIENTS

½ iceberg lettuce

150g rocket

2 small lebanese cucumbers

4 vine ripened tomatoes

3 shallots

8 kalamata olives

4 tbsp exra virgin olive oil

1 tbsp white wine vinegar

sea salt

cracked black pepper

METHOD

Cut lettuce in half lengthways and remove outer dark green leaves. Wash under cold running water then pat dry with paper towel. Cut in half again then slice across into 4cm slices. Place in salad bowl with rocket. Cover with cling film and allow to chill in the refrigerator while you cut remaining vegetables. Cut cucumber into 1/4 then across in 2cm dice. Dice the tomatoes the same way. Slice the shallots on the diagonal using the white plus green tops. Add salad vegetables with olives to lettuce and keep chilled until ready to serve.

TO MAKE THE DRESSING

Whisk the oil and vinegar together. Add salt and pepper. Pour over salad just before serving and toss well.

Note: for a quick lunch add cooked prawns, roasted chicken breast or tuna chunks and serve with crusty bread.

Serves 4.

There is nothing special about this salad but I am always asked to make "my special salad". Traditionally, lettuce should be torn - I like to cut it. Maybe that's the difference.

I call these meat rissoles "Cassie" Keftethes, as the ingredients and size differ to rissoles made in other parts of Greece.

CASSIE-KEFTETHES

INGREDIENTS

KEFTETHES

500g premium mince steak

1 large ripe tomato grated

1 large brown onion grated

¼ cup finely chopped mint

1 tbsp water

4 tbsp flour

1 tsp salt, ground pepper

extra flour for coating

oil for frying

TOMATO RELISH

4 ripe tomatoes

1 red onion

fresh mint

juice of 1 lime

SALAD

1 large cucumber

1 purple onion

12 kalamata olives

250g feta cheese

juice of 1 lemon

½ cup extra virgin olive oil

freshly ground black pepper

METHOD

KEFTETHES: Mix together meat, tomato, onion and mint in a bowl. Add water and flour, salt and pepper and mix again combining well. Shape into balls using about a heaped soup spoon of mixture for each. Roll in flour and cook in batches in hot oil (about 1cm deep). Flatten each gently with the back of a fork.

Fry for 3 minutes then turn over and finish cooking on the other side. Drain on kitchen paper then transfer to a serving plate.

Serves 4.

Note: Keftethes are delicious served with a tomato relish and a salad of sliced purple onion, cucumber, black olives and crumbled feta with an oil and lemon dressing.

TOMATO RELISH: Remove skins and seeds from tomatoes. Cut tomatoes and onion into very small dice. Add chopped mint. Pour over lime juice.

SALAD: Cut cucumber in half lengthways. Scoop out seeds and slice on the diagonal. Cut onion in half and thinly slice. Add olives and crumbled feta. Pour over olive oil and lemon juice.

GREEK ROAST LAMB AND LEMON POTATOES

INGREDIENTS

LAMB

1-2kg leg lamb

juice and zest of 1 lemon

2 tsp olive oil

2 cloves garlic peeled and sliced lengthways into 6 pieces

½ bunch fresh oregano leaves picked off stems

sea salt and ground black pepper

½ cup water

LEMON POTATOES

1kg large waxy potatoes cut into quarters lengthways

1 tbsp dried oregano

extra virgin olive oil

juice of 2 lemons

salt

METHOD

LAMB: Make 6 incisions in lamb and stuff with garlic wrapped in oregano leaves. Combine lemon juice, zest, olive oil, remainder of oregano, salt and pepper and rub all over lamb. Place meat into a roasting pan. Pour water into the bottom of pan. Roast in a hot oven for 1 hour. Allow to rest before carving.

LEMON POTATOES: Preheat the oven to 200°C. Arrange the potatoes in an oven proof dish. Season with salt and oregano. Add olive oil and lemon juice, pour over sufficient water to cover the potatoes. Bake in the preheated oven until water has evaporated. To brown the top, drizzle with more olive oil. When brown, turn off the oven and leave in the oven to stand for a few minutes.

KOULOURAKIA

INGREDIENTS

4 cups/ 500g plain flour

2 tsp baking powder

1½ tsp ground cinnamon

¼ tsp ground cloves

¼ tsp ground nutmeg

1 cup/200g sugar

1 generous cup / 250mls Greek extra virgin olive oil

1 tbsp brandy

3 tbsp + 1 tsp mineral water

3 tbsp + 1 tsp orange juice

1 tsp orange zest

sesame seeds for decoration

METHOD

Preheat oven to 180°C.

Sift the flour and baking powder into a bowl. Mix in the cinnamon, cloves and nutmeg.

Using the high setting on a blender, mix together the sugar, olive oil, brandy, mineral water, orange juice and orange zest until sugar has dissolved (about 2 minutes).

Add this sugar mixture to the flour in the bowl and knead all the ingredients together to form a smooth dough.

Taking one piece of dough at a time, roll it into thumb-thick sausages of pastry about 10cm long. Press the ends together firmly to make rings, plaits or other shapes.

Dip tops onto sesame seeds and spread out shapes on a baking tray.

Bake in preheated oven for 20 minutes.

Makes about 48.

HALVA

HALVA

200g unsalted butter
1 cup sugar
5 eggs
2 cups semolina (1 tea cup
measure + 1 standard cup
measure - my secret)
1 cup self raising flour
3 level tsp baking powder
grated rind of 1 orange

SYRUP

3 cups sugar
4 cups water
1 slice of lemon

HALVA: To make cake: Cream butter, orange rind and sugar till light and fluffy, add eggs one at time until incorporated. Sift flour with baking powder twice, add semolina and fold into butter mixture. Spread into a baking dish 25cm x 35cm.

Bake in a moderate oven for 3/4 hour or until cooked (test with a skewer). Pour on the syrup. Allow to rest before cutting into pieces.

SYRUP: Place water in a saucepan with lemon and stir in sugar over heat until dissolved. Boil syrup for 10 minutes. Pour hot syrup gently over warm cake (use all syrup even though it appears to be too much).

LOUKOUMATHES

honey puffs

INGREDIENTS

30g fresh yeast

9 cups of flour

1 tsp sugar

oil for frying

honey

cinnamon

METHOD

In a bowl, knead a generous 2 cups/250g flour with the yeast, sugar and a little water into a smooth dough. If using active dry yeast, follow the manufacturer's instructions. Cover the bowl with a cloth and allow to rest in a warm place until the dough has doubled in volume.

Work in the remaining flour, adding water as needed to form a workable dough. Cover the bowl and allow the dough to rise again, this time for about 1½ hours, until no bubbles form on the surface.

Heat plenty of oil in a deep-fry pan. Using a spoon, scoop out little balls of dough and drop gently into the boiling oil. Fry the dough balls until they are crisp and golden brown. Remove the loukoumathes from the oil with a ladle and drain on paper towel.

Finally arrange the "Puftaloons" on a serving dish. Pour over plenty of honey and sprinkle with cinnamon.

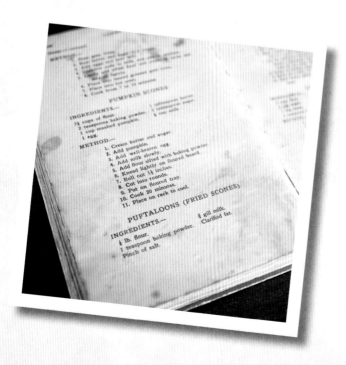

Today, Loukoumathes are probably better translated as Honey Puffs but my dad called them Puftaloons. Maybe he copied his recipe from my mother's "Commonsense Cookery Book, circa 1939.

I remember Dad had his own special technique for making Puftaloons. I call it the 'double thumb' method. He would take a large fist full of dough and with this special thumb technique he would push bits of the dough into the oil, using the index finger of his other hand to cut off just the right amount.

Every Kastellorizian has eaten Katoumari at some stage of their life. If not, then they are not a true Kastellorizian.

I have eaten Katoumari so many times and at least four times in Cassie. This recipe was given to me by my Aunty Irene who, like Dad, was born in Kastellorizio.

The tradition of making Katoumari is passed down through the generations. My grandchildren will be shown how to make this traditional sweet and hopefully they will pass it on to their children.

KATOUMARI

traditional kastellorizian pastry

INGREDIENTS

4 generous cups
of plain flour

1 pinch of salt

200ml warm water

500g unsalted butter

1 cup sugar

2 tsp ground cloves

METHOD

Sift flour and salt into a large bowl. Using your hands slowly add water to flour until all incorporated. Knead flour until a soft dough is formed. Break dough into 3 portions. Working with a portion at a time, roll out dough until very fine - stretching with your hands until paper thin and lay on to a floured surface (don't worry if holes appear).

Melt butter. Do not allow it to brown. Using a pastry brush, brush pastry generously with butter and at the same time roll pastry in to a long narrow roll, brushing with melted butter as you go. Gather ends and form a circle.

Heat a 30cm heavy based frying pan and brush with butter. Using a rolling pin flatten the circle to fit the pan snugly. Cook over medium heat until brown and then turn and cook other side. Do not allow to burn but make sure the dough is cooked well.

Remove from pan and sprinkle with a little water, sugar and ground cloves.

Pull apart and serve warm.

Makes 3.

Aunty Irene is
96 years old
and can still
make Katoumari
without any help.

MARY'S GALAKTOBOUREKO

mary's custard cake

INGREDIENTS

1 35cm x 25 cm sponge
(see recipe page 35)

SYRUP

1 cup sugar

1 cup water

1 cinnamon stick

squeeze of lemon

strip of lemon rind

CUSTARD FILLING

4 cups milk

¾ cups sugar

¾ cup fine semolina

grated rind of ½ lemon

1 cinnamon stick

¾ tsp salt

5 eggs lightly beaten

1 tsp vanilla essence

TO SERVE

500ml whipping cream

½ tsp vanilla essence

100g toasted almond flakes

METHOD

SYRUP: Place ingredients in a saucepan and stir over low heat until sugar dissolves. Bring to the boil and boil over moderate heat for 10 minutes. Strain and allow to cool.

CUSTARD: Bring milk, sugar, cinnamon stick, lemon rind and salt to the boil, stirring to dissolve sugar. Add semolina and cook gently, stirring often until thickened. Remove from heat and allow to cool. Blend in eggs and vanilla and cook again over low heat for a few minutes.

TO ASSEMBLE: Line a dish with half the sponge. Pour 1/4 cup of syrup on cake. Pour the warm custard on top of the moistened cake. Place the remaining sponge on top and pour another 1/4 cup syrup on top layer. Allow to cool completely. Smooth the cream that has been whipped with 1/2 teaspoon vanilla on the top. Sprinkle with toasted almond flakes.

My family has always loved my mother's Galaktoboureko. It's a little different to the traditional recipe. Mary preferred to use sponge instead of filo pastry and topped it off with whipped cream and toasted almonds.

Mum invented this version because she didn't like pastry. I like the traditional version too and you can usually find this version available in Greek delicatessens.

MARY'S GALAKTOBOUREKO
mary's custard cake

For celebrations the recipe quantities can be doubled to make a large cake just as we did here.

KOURABIETHES

shortbread cookies with icing sugar

INGREDIENTS

200g unsalted butter

3 tbsp icing sugar

1 tsp vanilla essence

1 tsp brandy

2 egg yolks

2 cups plain flour

½ tsp baking powder

whole cloves

icing sugar for dusting

METHOD

Beat butter and icing sugar with vanilla until light and creamy. Add egg yolks and brandy and beat well. Sift flour with baking powder twice. Mix lightly into butter mixture.

Roll out mixture in 2 batches to about 1cm thickness. Using a star biscuit cutter, cut out cookies. Push a clove in the centre of each one.

Place on nongreased baking tray and cook in a 180°C oven for 20 minutes. Cool cookies on a rack.

Sift icing sugar over baking paper and lift cookies onto this and sift more icing sugar over the top and sides.

Store in an airtight container.

Makes 24 approx.

Throughout my many holidays to Greece I have noticed that breakfast traditionally comprises a Greek coffee and a slice of cake, or Paximadia.

Many of my friends love Sunday breakfasts at their favourite cafe. As Andy and I spend so much time at our favourite 'Cafe' (Il Centro), we usually take the time to enjoy Sunday morning breakfast on our balcony at home, overlooking the wonderful city of Brisbane. We take turns making breakfast.

I love the Australian culture of a bacon and egg breakfast, but with a Greek twist. However, when it's Andy's turn, he buys pastries from the French Patisserie in New Farm!

POACHED ORGANIC EGGS

with crispy bacon, rocket,
tomato and feta

INGREDIENTS

4 organic eggs

4 rashes of bacon

1 roma tomato

handful of rocket (organic peppery rocket from farmer's market)

20g Greek feta

extra virgin olive oil

juice of ½ lemon

toasted sourdough

METHOD

Fry bacon rashes till crisp. Dice roma tomato. Tear rocket. Crumble feta.

Poach eggs in simmering water for 5 minutes so white is set and yolk is soft. Toss the rocket, tomato and feta together and add the oil and lemon juice. Drain the bacon on kitchen paper. Place poached eggs on toasted sourdough. Add salad and bacon.

Season with sea salt and cracked pepper.

Serves 2.

In 1969 I married Andy, the accountant. After seeing the hours my father worked, I loved the fact Andy worked a 9 to 5 job. But to my initial surprise, Andy's regular hours weren't to last.

My father could see the potential in his new son-in-law and in 1972 we moved from Sydney to Brisbane and Andy purchased from Michael the Cubana Coffee Lounge and Camelia Restaurant in partnership with George Tambakis.

So now, Andy became a restaurateur with a staff of about 70 and I was a stay-at-home mum. By 1974 our family had increased to four.

Because of my passion for cooking, our children Darren and Samantha were introduced to a varied and sophisticated diet at a very young age.

In the early 1970s it was customary for most young married couples with children to entertain at home.

Whenever Andy was not working we would often have 6 to 8 people over for dinner. I loved entertaining.

I was a good cook and my friends would always say,
"Why don't you open your own restaurant?" I would
laugh because I knew it was one thing to cook for
6 to 8 people, and a very different thing to cook for
60 to 80 paying customers. And besides we had the
wonderful Cubana.

I particularly remember on one occasion inviting 10
people over for dinner and telling them I was not
very fond of the traditional entree- main-dessert
format. Instead, I informed them that I would be
serving several small courses.

My wonderfully supportive husband, Andy, spent a
couple of hundred dollars purchasing champagne,
sherry, vodka, red, white and dessert wines and
liqueurs - each of which would accompany a
different course.

The dinner was a great success.
A degustation menu was created... and
I didn't even know the word existed!

As the years passed, Brisbane saw many
fabulous restaurants open their doors. Andy
and I would eat out as often as we could.

By this time we had sold the Camelia and
Andy would share the hours with George at
the ever popular Cubana.

But all good things must come to an end, and
after 20 successful years it was time for us to
move on.

ITALIAN BY HEART

By the early 90s, the time had come for Andy and I to open
the restaurant we always talked about. Because of my love of
anything Italian, especially Italian food, I felt our new venture
had to be an Italian restaurant.

We found the perfect location by the river in the heart of Brisbane
and assembled a terrific team of about 20 staff. I certainly did not
possess the skills (or confidence) to cook for more than 10 people
at once, so we also found a great chef.

And on 3 April 1992 we officially opened Il Centro Restaurant and
Bar at Eagle Street Pier.

And I'm very proud to say, after two successful decades, we're
still going strong!

In this section of my book, I'd like to share with you some of the
most popular dishes served at Il Centro.

BEEF CARPACCIO

with horseradish mousse, fried baby capers and black pepper tuile

INGREDIENTS

400g piece of eye fillet

25ml extra virgin olive oil

1 red onion finely diced

3 tbsp of baby capers

wild rocket leaves for garnish

60g goat's curd

100m double cream

½ gelatin leaf soaked in cold water

20g fresh horseradish

salt and pepper

TUILE

40g butter

40g plain flour

40g egg white

salt and cracked pepper

METHOD

Heat goat's curd in a small pan. Add gelatin leaf. Cool over an iced water bath. Whip cream until thick and fold into curd mix. Add horseradish, salt and pepper to taste. Allow to set in a bowl.

Slice the beef paper thin (best done when slightly frozen).

Place sliced beef onto a flat plate and cover each slice with cling film until ready to use. This will prevent oxidization.

TO SERVE: Remove cling film from beef. Brush with extra virgin olive oil. Season with salt and cracked pepper. Sprinkle the onion and baby capers around plate. Quenelle a dessert spoon of mousse mix in the centre (use a hot spoon to get a good result). Place one tuile on top of the mousse. Garnish with rocket leaves.

Serves 4.

TUILE: Mix the melted butter and flour together. Beat egg whites to a soft peak and fold into flour mixture. Cut a piece of baking paper 10cm x 2cm for each tuile. Spread a thin layer of the mix onto the paper. Bake in a moderate oven for 2 minutes. While still hot, carefully peel off paper and curl around a rolling pin until cool. Repeat curling process until all done.

HOUSE CURED
TASMANIAN SALMON

with scampi ravioli and blood orange dressing

INGREDIENTS

SALMON

1x side of salmon skin on, pin boned

½ bunch thyme

375g sugar

750g salt

zest of 1 orange

zest of 1 lemon

PASTA DOUGH

250g 00 flour

1 egg

110g infused saffron water

olive oil

RAVIOLI FILLING

250g scampi meat

½ brown onion diced

1 garlic clove peeled, chopped finely

2 tbsp mascarpone

2 stalks Italian parsley

salt and white pepper

20ml extra virgin olive oil

BLOOD ORANGE DRESSING

300ml blood orange puree

60ml aperol liquor

extra virgin olive oil

METHOD

SALMON: Trim belly off salmon. Line a container with cling film. Combine sugar, salt, zest and thyme and place half on the cling film. Place salmon into container and place remainder of salt mix on top of salmon. Wrap tightly and sit in the refrigerator for 24 hours. Unwrap, rinse with cold water. The salmon is now ready to slice.

TO SERVE: Cut the salmon into thin slices. Layer the outside of the plate with salmon. Place one or two ravioli into the middle of the plate. Spoon a generous amount of dressing over salmon. Garnish with petite asparagus and herb salad if desired.

Serves 4.

PASTA DOUGH: Blend all together in a food processor until combined. Knead lightly on a floured bench. Let rest in the fridge for ½ hour before rolling out in pasta dough machine. Cut dough into 7-8cm rounds.

RAVIOLI FILLING: Heat a nonstick pan. Add the oil and saute the scampi meat. Put aside. Using the same pan, fry the onion and garlic until the onion is transparent. It is important that the onion and garlic are cooked well. Add the scampi. Season with salt and pepper. Once the mixture has cooled down, add the mascarpone cheese and chopped parsley. To assemble the ravioli, allow approximately 40g of mixture to each one.

BLOOD ORANGE DRESSING: Place puree in a pan over medium heat and reduce to half (150ml). Add aperol liquor and emulsify with olive oil.

GRILLED KING PRAWN CUTLETS

with preserved lemon, mascarpone risotto and fresh peas

INGREDIENTS

12 green prawns peeled with tail on

1 tbsp olive oil

250g carnaroli rice

375ml vegetable stock

75ml white wine

1 small onion

5g garlic

200g fresh peas

20ml olive oil

25g butter

whisked mascarpone

preserved lemon

parmesan cheese

salt and pepper

METHOD

Heat olive oil in a pan. Add prawns and grill 6 at a time until golden brown. Put on a tray and keep warm. In a saucepan add diced onion and garlic with olive oil. Saute until translucent. Add rice and preserved lemon. Make sure rice is well coated with the oil and preserved lemon. Add hot vegetable stock and white wine. Bring back to the boil and simmer stirring often for 20 minutes. When rice is cooked add the butter, parmesan, peas and mascarpone. Risotto should be creamy.

TO SERVE: Remove the tails from 8 prawns and add the prawns to the risotto. Divide risotto between 4 serving bowls. Garnish each one with the remaining prawns.

Serves 4.

ORECCHIETTE PASTA

*with baccala, grilled zucchini flowers,
fresh chilli and garlic*

INGREDIENTS

400g orecchiette pasta

4 pieces of salt cod, cut
from the thick central parts
of the fish

extra virgin olive oil

2 cloves garlic sliced

fresh chilli julienne

50ml white wine

ground white pepper

8 zucchini flowers

METHOD

Blend all herbs, anchovies and capers. Cook pasta in a saucepan of
boiling water until al dente. Grill salt cod. Saute garlic and chilli in
olive oil until soft. Add white wine and simmer gently. Season with
white pepper. Toss through pasta and place grilled, flaked baccala
on top. Add one or two zucchini flowers which have been
char-grilled.

Serves 4.

ANGEL HAIR PASTA

*with sauteed king crab, scallops, snow peas,
sweet garlic and citrus salsa*

INGREDIENTS

8 prawns

8 scallops

200g king crab

400g angel hair pasta

½ bunch sweet basil

½ bunch chives

200g snow peas

16–20 cherry tomatoes

1 tbsp olive oil

salt and pepper

INGREDIENTS

50g roasted garlic cloves

25g diced lemon zest

25g fresh chilli diced

250ml white wine

25ml lemon juice

180ml extra virgin olive oil

METHOD

Shell and clean seafood. Put in the refrigerator until needed. Cut cherry tomatoes in half and place on a baking tray with rock salt. In a 150°C oven, allow the tomatoes to dry out. Blanch snow peas then refresh in iced water and cut lengthways into thin slices. In the meantime bring a large pot of water to the boil. Using a nonstick frying pan, add olive oil and cook prawns until golden. Add the scallops and brown quickly then toss through crab meat. Add the garlic and lemon salsa to the pan to coat seafood. Add snow peas, tomatoes and fresh herbs. When water is boiling, cook pasta for a few minutes, then strain into a colander.

TO SERVE: Toss the pasta through the seafood mix. Add a little more garlic and lemon salsa. Check seasoning. Divide between plates.

Serves 4.

SWEET GARLIC AND CITRUS SALSA: Peel and finely chop the garlic. Reduce the wine by half to 125ml. In a separate pan saute chilli and garlic in 30ml of oil. Add the lemon juice and rind, then wine. Bring to the boil and add the remaining oil.

FETTUCCINE

with wild mushroom ragout, truffle cream, rocket and shaved parmesan

INGREDIENTS

400g fettuccine

4 punnets of assorted mushrooms

80ml extra virgin olive oil

2 cloves of garlic

2 eschallots

15g truffle pesto

300ml thickened cream

salt and cracked black pepper

shaved parmesan

rocket leaves

PASTA

275g 00 flour

3 egg yolks

2 whole eggs

pinch salt

20ml olive oil

METHOD

Finely slice the mushrooms. Chop garlic and finely dice eschallots. Saute all mushrooms separately in a large nonstick pan using a small amount of olive oil each time. Use a high heat. Doing this will avoid mushrooms from stewing. Put mushrooms to the side reserving all the juices from the pan. Fry the eschallots and garlic until transparent. Add the truffle pesto and reserved mushroom juices. Bring to the boil, add the cream and reduce for 5 mins. Add all the mushrooms back to the pan. Toss the mushroom mixture through fettuccine and garnish with rocket and parmesan.

Serves 4.

PASTA: Beat eggs together. Sift the flour onto a clean surface and form a well. Pour the eggs into the centre. Using a fork, gradually mix the eggs and flour together. Once combined, add the salt and oil and knead gently until pasta dough becomes smooth. Wrap in cling film and rest in the refrigerator for at least 30 mins. Once rested, pass through pasta machine and continue rolling until the 1.5 mark. Pass through fettuccine attachment. Place pasta onto a lightly floured tray until ready to cook. Makes enough pasta for four.

Since opening, we've had four Executive Chefs. Our current Chef, Catherine Anders took over the mantle in June 2010.

Catherine first joined us a Sous Chef but since being promoted has become an amazing asset to our business, running an efficient, happy and relaxed kitchen.

Like many businesses in Brisbane, the summer of 2011, coupled with the GFC, really tested our mettle. We were very fortunate to be spared from the worst of the flood damage that affected many other restaurants along the river.

And thanks to the hard work and dedication of our kitchen brigade, front of house staff and senior management, we've continued to take pleasure in serving great numbers of diners each day.

Il Centro's famous
SAND CRAB LASAGNE
with creamed crustacean sauce

INGREDIENTS

LASAGNE

20-25 lasagne sheets

1.5 kg crab meat

90ml Napoli sauce (use ready made sauce for this small amount)

BÉCHAMEL

1.7lt milk

225g butter

235g plain flour

20ml lemon juice

50g tomato paste

Sea salt and white pepper

CRUSTACEAN SAUCE

300ml fish stock

1lt thickened cream

*100g ricci marini

62g tomato paste

Sea salt and white pepper

*ricci marini - Sea Urchin Roe
available from speciality delicatessen

METHOD: Heat the crab meat in a little butter, making sure it is hot ready to add to the béchamel.

TO MAKE THE BÉCHAMEL: Bring milk to boil over low heat. In a seperate pan melt the butter. Stir in the flour to make a roux (cook until a sandy texture). Add the milk slowly with a whisk and stir until sauce thickens. Season with salt and pepper and add lemon juice. You will need to divide sauce up before adding the crab, remove 600g of the béchamel and put into a bowl with the tomato paste; this is the topping for your lasagne (use a hand blender to keep smooth).

Add crab to remaining sauce ensuring there is no extra liquid, mix together well. This will now have to be divided into 3 equal parts (approx 750g each) for your layers.

TO ASSEMBLE THE LASAGNE: Spread the bottom of a 35cm x 20cm baking dish with the Napoli sauce. Layer the lasagne sheets over the sauce. Place the first lot of the crab mix into the dish. Cover with another layer of lasagne sheets. Repeat process twice using the remaining crab, ending with lasagne sheets. For the final layer spread the tomato paste/béchamel on the top. Cook in a 160°C oven for 40 mins. Allow to rest covered with foil for 10 mins before serving.

CRUSTACEAN SAUCE: In a saucepan, add 10ml olive oil. Add the tomato paste and ricci marini. Cook for 2 min. Add the fish stock and bring to boil. Once boiled, mix with a hand blender then strain through a fine strainer. Place back into another pot and add the cream. Bring to the boil. Season with salt & pepper.

TO SERVE: Cut the lasagne into serving pieces and spoon the desired amount of hot sauce over each serve.

Serves 12 entreé, 6 main

MORETON BAY BUG TAILS

with potato gnocchi, young fennel,
tomato and hazelnut butter

INGREDIENTS

MORETON BAY BUG TAILS

8 green bugs

16 cherry tomatoes

12 green asparagus spears

3 baby fennel cut into 6
pieces

50ml extra virgin olive oil

50g butter

12 sage leaves

80–100ml vegetable stock

zest of ½ lemon

650g potato gnocchi

GNOCCHI

600g dutch cream potatoes

100g semolina

70g plain flour

70g parmesan

1 egg

2 egg yolks

extra 50g plain flour

METHOD

MORETON BAY BUG TAILS: Cut the bugs in half and clean thoroughly. Place in boiling water and cook for 3–4 minutes. Once cool, remove bug meat from shell and set aside. Cut cherry tomatoes in half. Place on baking tray with rock salt and in 150°C oven, allow the tomatoes to dry out. Blanch and refresh the asparagus and fennel. Cool the asparagus and cut in half. Heat the oil in a nonstick pan and brown fennel each side. Remove from pan. Repeat with the gnocchi and bug meat then remove from pan. Add butter to pan and heat until butter has a nutty aroma. Put all the ingredients back into the pan. Add vegetable stock and emulsify. Cook gnocchi in a pot of boiling water. When gnocchi floats to the top remove from pot. Crisp sage leaves in hot oil.

TO SERVE: Put the gnocchi in the centre of the plate. Place bugs on top and arrange the asparagus and fennel around the plate. Garnish with crispy sage leaves.

Serves 4.

GNOCCHI: Cook potatoes in their skin at 180°C for 20–30 mins. Scrape out insides and put through a drum sieve. Put into metal bowl, this will keep the potatoes warm. Add semolina, flour, parmesan and eggs. Knead together to make a firm dough. Sprinkle extra flour onto a clean bench surface. Roll gnocchi into a sausage like form about 2cm diameter then cut into 2cm pieces. Roll in the palm of your hand to form a quenelle shape. Place on a floured tray ready for cooking. Makes 1kg of gnocchi.

DUCK BREAST

*with celeriac panna cotta, pea ragout,
pear and marsala jus*

INGREDIENTS

4 duck breast

190ml cream

1 egg and 1 egg yolk

3 french eschallots diced

200g fresh peas

2 slices prosciutto

2 cloves garlic crushed

30ml sherry vinegar

400ml beef stock reduced
to half

100ml marsala reduced
to half

2 pears

CELERIAC PANNA COTTA

30ml olive oil

1kg celeriac (peeled and cut
into 1cm cubes)

1 brown onion, diced

500ml thickened cream

500ml full cream milk

Salt and pepper

METHOD

Cook duck breasts in pan over low heat until pink. Season with salt and pepper and rest in a warm place. Boil the cream add the whisked eggs and hot celeriac puree. Place 4 molds in baking pan filled with a little water. Bake at 150°C for 30 minutes. Saute 2 eschallots, garlic and prosciutto in olive oil then deglaze with sherry vinegar. Add peas and a touch of water and season. In olive oil saute the remaining eschallots. Deglaze with marsala add stock and simmer slowly for 10 mins to obtain a syrupy sauce. Poach pears till golden and cut into quarters.

TO SERVE: Place sliced duck breast, panna cotta and pea ragout on a plate. Pour around marsala jus and place sliced pear on top.

Serves 4.

CELERIAC PANNA COTTA: Sweat onions in a pot till translucent, add celeriac and fry for 5 mins stirring occasionally. Add the milk and cream and bring to the boil. Turn down heat and simmer until celeriac is tender. Process the celeriac, milk and cream in a blender until smooth. Season with salt and pepper to taste.

CHAR-GRILLED EYE FILLET

*with gorgonzola frittata, roasted baby beets
and red wine jus*

INGREDIENTS

4 x 200g eye fillet

12 garlic cloves

20ml olive oil

salt and pepper

500g spinach

Gorgonzola frittata

2 bunches baby beetroot

500mls white vinegar

1 tbsp honey

100ml balsamic vinegar
plus 20ml extra

2 tbsp brown sugar

GORGONZOLA FRITTATA

1kg potatoes

2 brown onions

3 eggs

250ml cream

100g Gorgonzola cheese

20ml olive oil

salt and pepper

METHOD

Bring white vinegar, balsamic and honey to the boil. Add beetroot and allow to poach gently for 1 hour. Allow to cool then using gloves, remove the skin by rubbing gently. Cut each beetroot into quarters. Heat olive oil in a pan, add the brown sugar and caramelise. Add the extra balsamic. Season with salt and pepper and keep warm. Preheat oven to 180°C. Heat olive oil in a fry pan and sear fillet each side for 2 minutes. Add garlic to pan and place into the oven with steak for 8 minutes. Let steak rest for at least 5 minutes before serving. Wilt down the spinach in a little olive oil.

TO SERVE: Heat the frittata in the oven for 10 minutes while steak is cooking. Cut into 5cm squares. Place a square of frittata in the centre of each plate. Add the wilted spinach and steak. Arrange garlic and beets around plate. Finish with red wine jus. Season.

Serves 4.

GORGONZOLA FRITTATA: Slice onions finely. Heat oil in pan and fry onions slowly until golden and soft. Sprinkle onions with a little salt while cooking to stop them from breaking down. Slice potatoes very thin using a mandolin. Place in a saucepan of cold water and bring to the boil. When half cooked remove and strain immediately. In a separate pan bring the cream and cheese to a boil. Whisk eggs until blended and add to the cream mixture. In a tray approx 20cm x 15cm, layer potatoes with onions and cover with the cream mixture. Cook for 45 minutes at 160° C. When cooked cover with another tray and place a weight on top until cool.

GRILLED BARRAMUNDI

*with dutch cream potato mash,
globe artichokes with balsamic onions
and salsa verde*

INGREDIENTS

BARRAMUNDI
1kg barramundi fillets
(skin on cut into 4 pieces)
20ml olive oil
sea salt and pepper
salsa verde
20g melted butter
20ml vegetable stock

POTATO MASH
600g dutch cream potatoes
40g melted butter
20ml olive oil
100ml cream
salt and pepper

ARTICHOKES
2 globe artichokes
12 small french escallots
1 clove garlic sliced
1 cup vegetable stock
20g brown sugar
60ml balsamic vinegar
40ml olive oil

SALSA VERDE
½ bunch basil
½ bunch mint
½ bunch italian parsley
6 brown anchovies
1 tbsp large capers
zest of 1 lemon
½ cup olive oil

METHOD

BARRAMUNDI: Season barramundi fillets with salt and pepper. Heat olive oil in a frying pan and fry fillets skin side down till lightly coloured. Put pan in the oven and cook for 8 minutes (ote do not turn the fish, keep it cooking skin side down as this will make the skin crispy). Remove from the oven and turn over. Allow it to rest in the pan until ready to serve.

TO SERVE: Blend salsa verde with the melted butter and vegetable stock. Put some salsa verde on a plate. Place a quenelle of potato mash in the centre of the plate and arrange globe artichokes and balsamic onions neatly around mash. Place the fish on top of mash.

Serves 4.

DUTCH CREAM POTATO MASH: Boil potatoes until soft then pass through a mouille. Using a whisk, beat in the melted butter and olive oil. Add in boiled cream. Season with salt and pepper.

GLOBE ARTICHOKES WITH BALSAMIC ONIONS: Cut 3/4 of stalk off artichoke. Remove outer leaves until leaves become soft. Cut each artichoke into 6. Remove inner core (this is the furry bit in the middle). In a small pan heat half the olive oil and saute whole eschallots and sliced garlic. Add vegetable stock and bring to the boil. Simmer until soft. Remove artichokes and eschallots from pan and place on a paper towel. Heat remaining olive oil in a frying pan and brown artichokes and eschallots. Remove artichokes from pan and add brown sugar to eschallots and caramelise slightly. Deglaze the pan with balsamic vinegar and cook until the eschallots become sticky.

SALSA VERDE: Pick herbs from stems and rinse. In a food processor, blend all herbs, anchovies, capers, lemon zest and oil to a pesto consistency.

COLD SET CALLEBAUT CHOCOLATE TART

*with mascarpone gelato
and strawberry sorbet*

INGREDIENTS

1 pastry shell 34cm x 11cm

240g double cream

1 ½ tbsp sugar

90g unsalted butter

350g dark Callebaut chocolate

75ml cold milk

STRAWBERRY SORBET

112g sugar

37g liquid glucose

60ml water

500g frozen strawberries

PASTRY

340g plain flour

150g unsalted butter, softened

90g icing sugar

2 eggs

1 tbsp vanilla

METHOD

Boil cream, sugar and salt together. Add chocolate and butter. Once the mixture has cooled, add the cold milk. Pour into the tart shell and allow to set in the refrigerator for 2 hours.

Serves 6 to 8.

STRAWBERRY SORBET: Mix all ingredients together in a pot and bring to the boil. Blend with a hand blender. Put through a strainer to remove all the seeds. Pour into an ice cream churner for 15 minutes. Remove and place in a container to freeze.

MASCARPONE GELATO: Refer to vanilla ice cream recipe page 35. Add 100g mascarpone cheese to the cream mixture.

PASTRY: Process the flour, butter, sugar and vanilla together until combined. Add the eggs and pulse until the mixture resembles a crumble texture. Turn the dough onto a lightly floured surface and knead lightly. Wrap in cling film and refrigerate for 1 hour. Roll pastry into a rectangle shape to fit a 34cm x 11cm dish. Make sure to pinch the sides of the shell to rise above the tin to allow for shrinkage. Refrigerate for another 15 minutes before baking. Line the tart base with baking paper and rice. Blind bake for 15 minutes at 150°C. Remove paper and rice and prick the shell with a fork. Brush with egg wash and bake for a further 10 minutes at the same temperature. Allow to cool before adding chocolate mixture.

BANANA BREAD AND BUTTER PUDDING

with poached fruits and malt gelato

INGREDIENTS

2 eggs

2 egg yolks

375ml milk

½ vanilla pod

75g sugar

1 banana bread

syrup

poached fruits

malt gelato

BANANA BREAD

4 tbsp unsalted butter

1 cup of castor sugar

2 eggs

3 tbsp milk

1 ½ cups self raising flour

½ tsp bi carb soda

3 bananas

SYRUP

1 tbsp honey

600ml dark rum

POACHED FRUITS

4 small paradise pears

8 fresh dates

1 small jar of macerated prunes

1 cinnamon quill

1 star anise

1l water

500g sugar

150ml lemon juice

METHOD

BREAD AND BUTTER PUDDING: Bring milk to the boil with vanilla. Whisk eggs and sugar together. Add the egg mixture to the milk and stir to combine. Strain through a sieve. Dice the banana bread into 2cm pieces. Grease 6 pudding molds. Line the molds with banana bread. Pour custard mix into the molds. Place them into a baking tray and fill the tray with water half way up the side of the molds. Bake in oven at 130°C for 25 minutes. Turn out puddings and pour over syrup. Serve them with poached fruits and malt gelato.

Serves 6.

BANANA BREAD: Cream butter and sugar together. Dissolve soda in milk and mix with eggs, add mashed banana. Fold in the flour. Put into a greased loaf tin and bake at 180°C for 30–35 minutes.

SYRUP: Heat honey and rum together in a small pan.

POACHED FRUITS: Bring water, sugar, cinnamon, star anise and lemon to the boil. Peel and core pears and add to the liquid. Cook till ½ done then add dates and prunes. Cover with a cartouche. Simmer until cooked. Remove seeds from dates. Cool fruit in liquid.

MALT GELATO: Refer to Vanilla Ice Cream on page 35. Replace vanilla bean with 40g Malt Powder.

DAINTREE FOREST VANILLA BEAN BRÛLÉE

with passionfruit sorbet

INGREDIENTS

400ml double cream

40ml full cream milk

5 egg yolks

1 vanilla bean

70g sugar

2 tbsp raw sugar

passionfruit sorbet

fresh passionfruit pulp

PASSIONFRUIT SORBET

1kg frozen passionfruit puree

360g sugar

170g glucose

470ml water

METHOD

BRÛLÉE: Bind egg yolks and sugar together (just together). Add the boiled cream and milk that has been infused with vanilla bean. Skim away any froth and strain through a fine chinois. Pour into brûlée molds and cook at 98°C for 40 minutes.

TO SERVE: Once brûlée is cool sprinkle raw sugar. Using a blowtorch caramelise the sugar. Quenelle a scoop of sorbet to accompany the brûlée and use fresh passionfruit pulp to garnish.

Serves 6.

PASSIONFRUIT SORBET:

Defrost puree, blend and strain. Bring to the boil puree, sugar, glucose and water. Strain through a fine chinois. Cool over an iced water bath. Churn for 15 minutes in an ice cream churner. Remove and place in a container and put in the freezer till required. Makes 1 litre.

My daughter, Samantha is a fabulous cook. She is especially good at styling food on the plate. She can turn a simple salad into the most fabulously enticing dish. I'm not as talented as she is at doing this, so I especially wanted her to help plate the food for my book.

How wonderful to have someone as passionate about food as I am to help me. Sam doesn't live in Brisbane, so I cherish the times we have cooking together.

The love of cooking appears to run in our family. Each Saturday, when all the sporting activities are over, it's baking time at Sam's house. My granddaughters, Jemima and Cordelia, bake with their dad. I think Dan has learned to be a great pastry cook thanks to his beautiful and talented girls.

INDEX

GREEK BY HERITAGE

ITALIAN BY HEART

Marcia Georges

ISBN 9781922036582   Qty

RRP   AU$45.00   .....

Postage within Australia   AU$5.00   .....

TOTAL★ $_____

★ All prices include GST

Name:...

Address: ....

....

Phone:...

Email: ....

Payment: ❑ Money Order ❑ Cheque ❑ Amex ❑ MasterCard ❑ Visa

Cardholders Name:...

Credit Card Number: ....

Signature:...

Expiry Date: ....

Allow 7 days for delivery.

Payment to: Marzocco Consultancy (ABN 14 067 257 390)
PO Box 12544
A'Beckett Street, Melbourne, 8006
Victoria, Australia
admin@brolgapublishing.com.au

Publishing through a successful Australian publisher.
Brolga provides:

- Editorial appraisal
- Cover design
- Typesetting
- Printing
- Author promotion
- National book trade distribution, including sales, marketing and distribution through Macmillan Australia.
- International book trade distribution
- Worldwide e-Book distribution

For details and inquiries, contact:
Brolga Publishing Pty Ltd
PO Box 12544
A'Beckett St VIC 8006

Phone: 0414 608 494
admin@brolgapublishing.com.au
markzocchi@brolgapublishing.com.au
ABN: 46 063 962 443

Published by Brolga Publishing Pty Ltd
ABN 46 063 962 443

PO Box 12544, A'Beckett St, VIC, 8006, Australia
email: markzocchi@brolgapublishing.com.au

National Library of Australia Cataloguing-in-Publication entry
Designed and produced by Generator, Brisbane.
Printed book designed by Wanissa Somsuphangsri

    Author: Georges, Marcia.
    Title: Greek by heritage Italian by heart / Marcia Georges.
    ISBN: 9781922036582 (hbk.)
    Subjects: Georges, Marcia.
         Cooks--Australia--Biography.
         Cooking, Greek.
         Cooking, Italian.

Dewey Number: 641.5092
Printed in China